The Infamous Bachelor Party Playbook

Jeremy Warlen

<u>WARNING</u>

When you mix this book with adult beverages you will create awesome memories. There is some content in this book that is considered "bad" or "illegal." Don't let that get in the way of having a great time! Just Remember, You understand that you are doing all of this because of your own stupidity. I don't want any Brides calling me pissed off. It is all on you!

Have Fun!

Some Legal Shit

ISBN- 13: 978-1536927948

ISBN- 10: 1536927945

<u>RULES</u>

Each Player will sign and date each challenge they finish.

At the end of the game, you will add up the points to see who is the most Infamous at this Bachelor Party!

Bachelor Only Challenges

☐ 1) Empty 3 Shot Glasses in a row.

10 points
Name:

_____

Date:

_____

☐ 2) Photo with 2 ladies kissing you, one on each cheek.

15 points
Name:

_____

Date:

_____

☐ 3) Get a phone number from
a bartender of your choice.

15 points

Name:

_____

Date:

_____

☐ 4) Get at least 2 lipstick kisses
on your neck.

10 points

Name:

_____

Date:

_____

☐ 5) Get behind the bar and pour your own shots.

20 points

Name:

_____

Date:

_____

☐ 6) Shot Gun a Beer.

10 points

Name:

_____

Date:

_____

☐ 7) Attempt to chug the whole beer bong.

15 points

Name:

_____

Date:

_____

☐ 8) Find a Bride-to-Be & get a photo of you carrying her.

15 points

Name:

_____

Date:

_____

☐ 9) Do a body shot off a lady.
20 points, 30 points if it's a Bride-to-Be
Name:

_____

Date:

_____

☐ 10) Get someone to do a body shot off you.
20 points
Name:

_____

Date:

_____

☐ 11) Get a bra from a willing lady.

25 points, 35 points if or over Double D

Name:

_____

Date:

_____

☐ 12) Serenade an unsuspecting lady with a love song.

10 Points

Name:

_____

Date:

_____

☐ 13) Get a woman to spank you.

10 points, 25 points for bare ass

Name:

_____

Date:

_____

☐ 14) Have a woman slap you in the face.

15 points

Name:

_____

Date:

_____

☐ 15) Convince a stranger your bride is still a virgin.

10 points

Name:

_____

Date:

_____

<u>Group Challenges</u>

☐ 1) Get panties from a willing lady.

> **25 points, 30 points if it's a G String**

> Name:

> _____

> Date:

> _____

☐ 2) Do a Keg Stand

> **25 points**

> Name:

> _____

> Date:

> _____

☐ 3) Chug "The Boot."

(A glass that can hold 5 beers)

20 points

Name:

_____

Date:

_____

☐ 4) Take a Selfie with a cop.

10 points

Name:

_____

Date:

_____

☐ 5) Make out with someone older than 40.

25 points

Name:

_____

Date:

_____

☐ 6) Find a woman who can tie a cherry stem into a knot with her tongue.

15 points

Name:

_____

Date:

_____

☐ 7) Get a selfie in the Girls Restroom.

10 points, 15 points if girls take the selfie with you.

Name:

_____

Date:

_____

☐ 8) Be the First to Puke.

20 points

Name:

_____

Date:

_____

☐ 9) Everyone knows people pee in the pool. What will people think when you stand outside the pool and pee into it?

25 points for empty pool, 50 points for people in the pool

Name:

_____

Date:

_____

☐ 10) T.P. a cop car.

50 points

Name:

_____

Date:

_____

☐ 11) Run over the top of a cop car.

50 points

Name:

_____

Date:

_____

☐ 12) Get a picture in handcuffs.

15 points

Name:

_____

Date:

_____

☐ 13) Buy a lap Dance for The Bachelor

25 points

Name:

_____

Date:

_____

☐ 14) Get kicked out of a bar.

35 points

Name:

_____

Date:

_____

☐ 15) Go into a store and only buy a condom, lube and a cucumber or banana.

15 points

Name:

_____

Date:

_____

☐ 16) Find a lady willing to flash the bachelor.

25 points

Name:

_____

Date:

_____

☐ 17) Moon someone from the car you are all riding in.

10 points

Name:

_____

Date:

_____

☐ 18) Poop in public.

35 points

Name:

_____

Date:

_____

☐ 19) While riding down the road, Poop in the car with the whole group in it.

45 points

Name:

_____

Date:

_____

☐ 20) Do a flaming shot.

20 points

Name:

_____

Date:

_____

☐ 21) Teach a woman how to be an exotic dancer.

(Must at least get your shirt off)

25 points

Name:

_____

Date:

_____

☐ 22) Walk down the street in just underwear.

25 points

Name:

_____

Date:

_____

☐ 23) Walk around the bar with your ass out.

20 points

Name:

_____

Date:

_____

☐ 24) Find a good looking woman and do a belly shot off her.

25 points

35 points if Bride-To-Be

Name:

_____

Date:

_____

☐ 25) Get a woman to give you a condom

10 points

Name:

_____

Date:

_____

☐ 26) Eat a spoonful of mustard or Tabasco sauce.

20 points

Name:

_____

Date:

_____

☐ 27) Lean into a person like you're about to tell a secret and lick that persons ear.

15 points

Name:

_____

Date:

_____

☐ 28) Be the guy that buys the group Tequila Shots.

60 points

Name:

_____

Date:

_____

☐ 29) Massage a stranger's foot.

10 points

Name:

_____

Date:

_____

☐ 30) Get 2 women to sign your chest.

15 points

Name:

_____

Date:

_____

☐ 31) Swallow a spoonful of cinnamon.

50 points if achieved,

25 points if not.

Name:

_____

Date:

_____

☐ 32) Blow a kiss to every passing car for 2 minutes.

10 points

Name:

_____

Date:

_____

☐ 33) Find a couple about to walk into somewhere, hold the door for the lady, then hold your arm out in a "Stop" motion at the man & go into the building after his lady, Leaving him outside.

25 points

Name:

_____

Date:

_____

☐ 34) Ask "How much?" to a group of girls on the street.

20 points

Name:

_____

Date:

_____

☐ 35) Smell a random person and ask if they eat cheese.

15 points

Name:

_____

Date:

_____

☐ 36) Punch a guy.

20 points

Name:

_____

Date:

_____

☐ 37) Get punched by a guy.

30 points

Name:

_____

Date:

_____

☐ 38) Get a video of a cop saying "Fuck The Police."

50 points

Name:

_____

Date:

_____

☐ 39) Get a photo with a Senior Citizen flipping off the camera.

25 points

Name:

_____

Date:

_____

☐ 40) Drink a shot of your own piss.

40 points

Name:

_____

Date:

_____

☐ 41) Surprise Slap one of your friends.

10 points

Name:

_____

Date:

_____

☐ 42) Eat a page from this
book.

40 points

Name:

_____

Date:

_____

This Page Taste like a
Tofu Burger

This Page Taste Like Dick!

☐ 43) Buy a round of hard whiskey and drink like Gentlemen.

60 points

Name:

_____

Date:

_____

☐ 44) Rip your shirt off "Hulk Style" in public.

20 points

Name:

_____

Date:

_____

☐ 45) Find a public fountain,
and then take a dip.

40 points

Name:

_____

Date:

_____

☐ 46) Who brought Jager
Bombs to the party? You did!

60 points

Name:

_____

Date:

_____

☐ 47) Get punched in the dick by a female.

35 points

Name:

_____

Date:

_____

☐ 48) Find a stranger who happens to be your twin.

30 points

Name:

_____

Date:

_____

☐ 49) Get Arrested.

200 points

Name:

_____

Date:

_____

☐ 50) Who can get the most phone numbers! You will need proof that you got a number. Use the following page to keep track of your scores and to keep all the girls numbers, because after this wild night the Bachelor might still be a bachelor.

10 points per number

Player	Girl's Name	Girl's Phone Number

Player	Girl's Name	Girl's Phone Number

Use This Page To Add Up Each Players Points!

The Score Board

Winner: _____

Points: _____

2nd Place: _____

Points: _____

3rd Place: _____

Points: _____

4th Place: _____

Points: _____

5th Place: _____

Points: _____

6th Place: _____

Points: _____

7th Place: _____

Points: _____

8th Place: _____

Points: _____

9th Place: _____

Points: _____

10th Place: _____

Points: _____

11th Place: _____

Points: _____

12th Place: _____

Points: _____

I have hosted and been a part of a lot of fun and crazy parties. And I am very happy to have been a part of your Bachelor Night! I hope it was a lot of fun! Congratulations!

-Jeremy Warlen

Thanks For Playing-

The Infamous Bachelor Party Playbook

Love it or Hate it?
Please leave an honest
Review on Amazon.

#infamousbachelor
Tag Me on Instagram-
@JeremyWarlen

Made in the USA
San Bernardino, CA
19 June 2018